# Birthday

# Cupcakes

Written by Karen Ewbank Roberts

Illustrated by Mike Reed

MODERN CURRICULUM PRESS

## Program Consultants

Becky Dugan, *Teacher*
Brady Elementary School
Little Rock, Arkansas

Debra List, *Teacher*
Hansberry Child-Parent Center
Chicago, Illinois

Judy Stobbe, *Bilingual Teacher*
Alianza School
Watsonville, California

Wanda Tansil, *Teacher*
University Terrace School
Baton Rouge, Louisiana

*Executive Editor:* Dorrie Berkowitz

*Associate Project Editor:* Marcia Formichelli

*Design concept:* Lillie Caporlingua/BILL SMITH STUDIO

MODERN CURRICULUM PRESS
An imprint of Paramount Supplemental Education
250 James Street
Morristown, New Jersey 07960



ISBN: 0-8136-7979-6 (single copy) 0-8136-8519-2 (6-pack)

1 2 3 4 5 6 7 8 9 DP 99 98 97 96 95 94

This is the very best day
of the week.

I have birthday cupcakes for a class treat!

Oh, no!

A big bump made them PLOP!

My birthday cupcakes are a flop.

Now I am very sad.

102

My birthday cupcakes look very bad.

But they taste just fine,

even if they are a mess.

Birthday cupcakes are the best!